Recognizing Tone

D0033683

Middle

The Jamestown Comprehension Skills Series with Writing Activities

THIRD EDITION

JAMESTOWN PUBLISHERS

a division of NTC/CONTEMPORARY PUBLISHING GROUP
Lincolnwood. Illinois USA

ISBN: 0-8092-0151-8

Published by Jamestown Publishers,
a division of NTC/Contemporary Publishing Group, Inc.
©2000 NTC/Contemporary Publishing Group, Inc.,
8787 Orion Place, 4th floor Columbus, Oh 43240

7 8 9 10 11 GLO 12 11 10

INTRODUCTION

The Comprehension Skills Series has been prepared to help students develop specific reading comprehension skills. Each book is completely self-contained. There is no separate answer key or instruction manual. Throughout the book, clear and concise directions guide the student through the lessons and exercises.

The titles of the Comprehension Skills books match the labels found on comprehension questions in other Jamestown textbooks. The student who is having difficulty with a particular kind of question can use the matching Comprehension Skills book for extra instruction and practice to correct the specific weakness.

Each book in the Comprehension Skills Series is divided into five parts.

1. Explanation: Part One (p. 5) clearly defines, explains, and illustrates the specific skill. It begins with a Preview Quiz to get students thinking about the material that will be presented.

2. Instruction: Part Two (p. 9) offers an interesting and informative lesson presented in clear, readable language. This section also utilizes the preview technique introduced in Part One, which requires students to anticipate and respond to the subject matter.

3. Sample Exercise: Part Three (p. 18) consists of a sample exercise with questions. The sample exercise is designed to prepare students for the work required in the following section. Students should read and follow the instructions carefully. When they have finished the exercise, they should read the analysis following it. For each question, there is a step-by-step explanation of why one answer is correct, and why the others are not. Students are urged to consult the teacher if they need extra help before proceeding to Part Four.

4. Practice Exercises: Part Four (p. 23) contains twenty practice exercises with questions. Squares (■) bordering the exercises indicate the level of difficulty. The greater the number of squares, the greater the difficulty of the passage. Students are advised to read the instructions and complete the practice exercises thoughtfully and carefully.

5. Writing Activities: Part Five (p. 49) contains writing activities that help students apply the skills they have learned in earlier parts of the book. Students should read and follow the instructions carefully. Many activities encourage students to work together cooperatively. The teacher may want to discuss these activities in class.

Each book also contains an Answer Key, which can be found after the Writing Activities. Students can record their scores and monitor their progress on the chart following the Answer Key.

PART ONE

Understanding Tone

Preview Quiz 1

As a preview of what will be discussed in Part One, try to answer this question:

Tone is the author's attitude in a piece of writing. **What is the tone of a story most likely to reveal?**

a. the author's feelings

b. a character's past

c. events in the plot

Begin reading Part One to learn how authors use tone.

The Emotional Quality of Language

To understand what you read requires many skills. One of them is recognizing tone and responding to it. Tone is the author's attitude toward his or her subject or audience. A writer creates tone through the emotional quality of language. Tone reveals feelings, attitudes, and points of view. Authors create tone by carefully choosing and arranging words. When someone speaks, several factors help us tell whether the person is happy or angry.

- the sound of the person's voice
- the choice of words
- the pace of delivery

For example, imagine a foggy day. A person who feels happy might use the words *hushed* and *fluffy* to describe the fog. These words would show the person's happy frame of mind. So would the way he or she spoke them. However, a person who feels frightened might use the words *blinding* and *spooky* to describe the same fog on the same day. The frightened person's voice might quake. There would be no mistaking his or her feelings.

We experience many emotions. Besides feeling joy or fear, we may feel hate, love, or anger. Any feeling can be revealed through words as tone.

Emotions and Attitudes

As we show our feelings, we reveal our attitudes. We may approve of what we see. We may disapprove. We may accept life as it is. We may reject it. We may show sincerity, sarcasm, or tenderness. At other times, we may show toughness, gratitude, ingratitude, and so on.

Think about two people who have different views on the same issue. Let's say that one person thinks a planned power plant threatens the quality of life in her town. She's worried. Her tone shows that she is. The other person thinks that the plant will improve the town in the long run. She's optimistic. Her tone shows her optimistic attitude.

Thus, a bitter person uses a bitter or sarcastic tone. An understanding or sympathetic person uses a tone of understanding, pity, or sympathy. Attitudes are reflected in tone.

Points of View

Point of view may also be shown through tone. Your point of view is the position from which you view issues that concern you. The way you speak usually makes your point of view clear. If you are sure about an issue, your tone is firm. If it means a lot to you, your tone is strong. If you don't care, your tone is mild, even bored.

Similarly, writers show their positions and make their ideas clear through tone. But setting a tone is harder in writing than in speaking. Writers do not have the benefit of sound. They must choose words more carefully than speakers. Writers must also vary the lengths of sentences to show feelings, attitudes, and points of view.

───── Preview Quiz 2 ─────

As a preview of what will be discussed next, try to answer this question:

A writer wants to show that a person is plain and sincere. *What kind of sentence would the writer be likely to use?*

    a. long and difficult

    b. short and direct

    c. loose and wordy

Continue reading to discover the correct answer.

Sentence Rhythms and Tone

The following passage is the beginning of a story. As you read it, notice the tone.

> I'm tired. I'm more tired than I've ever been before. But I'm happy. I don't think I've ever been happier. To tell you the truth, I never thought I'd see the sun come up today. When the prairie fire turned on us last night, I thought, "This is it. This is the end of you, Jenny Daniels." But here I am, and I'm thankful. I know that I owe my life to two people I had never met before last night. Today I think of those two people as my best friends in the world. Let me tell you how it happened.

Notice that the opening comments are short, direct, and strong. They set a tone of sincerity. The narrator is telling about herself. Her feelings are personal and sincere. She is relieved and grateful. There is sincerity and gratitude in her statements. She writes as if she were speaking to the reader. Her tone creates a friendly relationship with the reader. Thus, we can say that the author gives the narrator (the character who tells the story) a simple, direct, and sincere attitude.

As you read, you will need to recognize tone. Your understanding of tone will affect your comprehension. Consider the tone carefully. Think about what it suggests. Decide what it implies about the author's and narrator's attitudes.

This book will help you improve your ability to recognize different tones in reading. In Part Two, you will explore the steps involved. You will also have an opportunity to put them into practice.

How Tone Is Revealed

As a preview of what will be discussed in Part Two, try to answer this question:

What is another name for the general feeling of a story?

   a. setting

   b. mood

   c. climax

Begin reading Part Two to learn more about tone and how it is revealed.

The purpose of this section is to develop the information you learned in Part One. We will discuss three main topics:

- how tone is revealed in literature
- how tone adds meaning to ideas
- how you can analyze tone in what you read

Tone and Mood

In short stories, novels, and plays, tone adds to the general feeling or mood. Mood is an important part of most stories. Mood is the general feeling or atmosphere of a story. Tone helps to create a mood that affects the reader's imagination and emotions. The mood may be *cheerful, gloomy,* or *scary.* It may be *exciting, eerie, cozy,* and so on. A mood may be developed directly through the tone of a description, as in the following examples.

- A fierce sun beat on us as we staggered over the sand.
- A gentle sun smiled on us as we strolled over the sand.

Mood and Character

Mood may also be created by the tone of a character's own words. The next passage offers two good examples. It is from "The Foreigner" by Sarah Orne Jewett.

The story is set in a small village in the late 1800s. A visitor to Dunnet Landing becomes friends with Mrs. Almira Todd, a well-known inhabitant of the seaside village.

One evening, at the end of August, in Dunnet Landing, I heard Mrs. Todd's firm footsteps crossing the small front entry outside my door, and her conventional cough which served as a herald's trumpet, or a plain New England knock, in the harmony of our fellowship.

"Oh, please come in!" I cried, for it had been so still in the house that I supposed my friend and hostess had gone to see one of her neighbors. The first cold northeasterly storm of the season was blowing hard outside. . . . I could hear that the sea was already stirred to its dark depths, and the great rollers were coming in heavily against the shore. One might well believe that Summer was coming to a sad end that night, in the darkness and rain and sudden access of autumnal cold.

From the way the visitor speaks, we understand his feelings. He feels sadness at the end of summer and afraid of the approaching storm. He is also very lonesome and welcomes the sound of Mrs. Todd. His tone is apprehensive and frightened. In contrast, Mrs. Todd's approach displays the air of a self-determined woman with purpose.

Summary

In fiction, tone is best shown by the author's artistic use of words. Writers choose their words to stir the reader's feelings and thoughts. They want the reader to feel love, hate, joy, sorrow, and so on. The best writers do not state emotions directly. They suggest them indirectly. They show them at work.

Preview Quiz 4

As a preview of what will be discussed next, try to answer this question:

What is the mood in the paragraph below?

It was too hot to catch your breath, too hot for birds to sing. The sky was without a cloud to soften the sun, the leaves hung limp from the trees, the grass crackled underfoot and turned to dust.

    a. oppressive and weary

    b. chilly and mysterious

    c. peaceful and serene

Continue reading to discover the correct answer.

Setting a Mood Through Word Choice

Story openings often set the tone and mood. Usually the tone set in the opening sentence grows as the story continues. The passage in Preview Quiz 4 is an example of a story opening that sets the tone and mood. The first sentence alone sets an oppressive, weary mood.

The author's choice of words helps create the mood. Notice "leaves hung limp from the trees." Notice also "grass crackled underfoot." These images help you see and hear the effects of the heat. They help set the mood.

Setting a Mood Through Sentence Length

Word choice is not the only factor. The length and flow of sentences also help to set tone and mood. Consider the sentences in the example. The long sentences suggest slow movement. The sentence length strengthens the mood of oppressive heat. Short, choppy sentences would set another mood. They might suggest action or suspense.

The following passage from *The Call of the Wild* by Jack London shows how sentence structure can create tone. This is the famous scene in which the dog Buck pulls a heavy sled alone.

Buck threw himself forward, tightening the traces with a jarring lunge. His whole body was gathered compactly together in the tremendous effort, the muscles writhing and knotting like live things under the silky fur. . . . The sled swayed and trembled, half-started forward. . . . One of his feet slipped, and one man groaned aloud. Then the sled lurched ahead in a rapid succession of jerks, though it never came to a dead stop again . . . half an inch . . . an inch . . . two inches. . . . The jerks diminished; as the sled gained momentum, he caught them up, until it was moving steadily along.

Notice how the writing works. In a short sentence, Buck throws himself forward.

Buck threw himself forward, tightening the traces with a jarring lunge.

In a long sentence, he gathers his strength.

His whole body was gathered compactly together in the tremendous effort, the muscles writhing and knotting like live things under the silky fur.

Then, in a short sentence, he gets the sled moving.

The sled swayed and trembled, half-started forward.

In another short sentence, he slips.

One of his feet slipped, and one man groaned aloud.

Next is a complicated sentence. The long beginning describes the sled's jerky motion.

Then the sled lurched ahead in a rapid succession of jerks, though it never came to a dead stop again . . .

The end of the sentence imitates the motion.

half an inch . . . an inch . . . two inches. . . .

In the last sentence, the sled's jerking ends. The sentence smooths out, too. It moves along like the sled.

The jerks diminished; as the sled gained momentum, he caught them up, until it was moving steadily along.

Preview Quiz 5 ────────────────

As a preview of what will be discussed next, try to complete this sentence:

The tone can also reveal the author's

   a. attitude toward the subject.

   b. past writing experience.

   c. plan for the plot.

Continue reading to discover the correct answer.

The Writer's Attitudes

Every writer has an attitude toward the subject and an attitude toward the audience. Expressing these attitudes is part of the writer's aim. Attitudes are a part of the total meaning.

Most writers express personal attitudes to arouse and maintain readers' interest. Attitudes also add a personal touch. For some authors, expressing attitudes is the main reason for their writing.

Attitudes Toward the Subject of the Writing

Certain subjects seem to suggest appropriate attitudes. Therefore, certain tones seem appropriate to them. We are likely to notice a tone that is different from what we expect.

A serious subject, like disease or death, is normally treated in a serious tone. Ordinarily, death is too painful a topic to treat lightly. Joking is usually out of place. This doesn't mean that humor is not possible with serious topics. In fact, there are many humorous treatments of death.

An author's attitude toward the subject of a piece of writing is likely to affect the tone. Sometimes the author is aware of the effect that an attitude has on tone. At other times the author may not be aware that his or her attitude has affected the tone.

Suppose that an author is writing about a person with many faults. The faults may be treated with gentle humor. They may also be treated with bitter sarcasm. The choice depends on the author's attitude toward the character who has these faults.

The problems that humanity must solve may be treated seriously by one author. Another may treat them humorously. It depends on the author's attitude. Topics in politics, religion, and education may also be handled any number of ways.

Shakespeare had an interesting attitude toward misfortune. He felt that people may joke about their own misery but not about another person's. A character in Shakespeare's *Romeo and Juliet* even makes a joke about his death wound. He says that it is not as deep as a well nor as wide as a church door but that it is big enough to serve its purpose. In literature, as in real life, humor may help people escape from pain.

The Author's Purpose for Writing

The author's purpose for writing also influences tone. Some authors want to amuse the reader. They write with a humorous tone. Some authors want to inform the reader. They present ideas seriously and factually. Some authors want to arouse sympathy in the reader. They develop an emotional or sentimental tone.

Preview Quiz 6

As a preview of what will be discussed next, try to answer this question:

Which of these books is likely to be written in a suspenseful tone?

   a. *Science for Modern Living*

   b. *The Care of Houseplants*

   c. *Midnight Murders*

Continue reading to conclude this lesson on tone.

Matching the Tone and the Audience

The writer's understanding of the audience influences tone. The writer's attitude toward the audience also influences tone. Why? The writer tries to tailor the tone to suit the audience. The age, intelligence, and education of the readers may have to be considered. Their interests, habits, and expectations may also have to be considered.

Suppose a writer is discussing health care in an article in the *Science for Modern Living* magazine. The article has been written for an audience of scientists. The tone of the writing is serious and formal. Suppose the article is later rewritten for a magazine that reaches people with a broader range of interests, such as *Reader's Digest*. The tone is certain to become much less formal.

Writers may also try to predict their readers' reactions. A reader expects suspense in a mystery called *Midnight Murders*, but wants direct advice in *The Care of Houseplants*. Sometimes, writers may feel that readers will disagree with their ideas. Then they may try to create a tone to "win the reader over." If writers expect readers to agree, they may be more relaxed. A writer may use any number of approaches. Each approach will result in a different tone.

Recognizing Tone** **17

Tone in Advertising

Advertisements present many examples of the way a writer's attitude toward the audience affects tone. The advertiser has one thing in mind: selling. To do this, the ad must catch and hold the reader's interest. Here tone is very important. One writer may decide to write in a friendly tone because he or she knows that people like to be treated in a friendly way. Another writer may decide to use a flattering tone. Advertisers know that people like flattery. We all like to hear how smart, clever, and talented we are. Still other advertisers use a combination of tones. We may be flattered first, then informed, and then persuaded to buy the product.

Summary

Tone is an important part of meaning. Tone helps ideas come to life. Tone allows the writer's personality to show. The reader who does not understand tone misses part of the message. To recognize and appreciate tone, do the following:

- Study the first sentence of each paragraph. It may set the tone.

- Study descriptions. Study lines spoken by characters.

- Notice words that suggest feelings, attitudes, and points of view.

- Notice the lengths of sentences.

- Decide what the author's purpose for writing is.

- Decide what the author's attitude toward the topic is.

- Decide what the author's attitude toward the readers is.

Good writing, like good music, is carefully composed. Each word, like each musical note, adds to the tone of the whole work. A skillful reader looks for clues that signal tone.

This lesson has been designed to help you identify the tone and mood of what you read. You should now have a clearer understanding of the subject. Try to apply this knowledge to the sample exercise in Part Three. Put your new understanding of tone and mood to work in everything you read.

PART THREE

Sample Exercise

The exercise on the next page is a sample exercise. It shows how you can put the information you have learned in Parts One and Two to use in reading.

The sample exercise also previews the twenty exercises that appear in Part Four. Reading the sample passage and answering the sample questions get you off to a good start.

The answers to all the questions are fully explained. Reasons are given showing why the correct answers are the best answers and where the wrong answers are faulty. The text also describes the thinking you might do as you work through the exercise correctly.

Complete the sample exercise carefully and thoughtfully. Do not go on to Part Four until you are certain that you understand what tone is and how to recognize tone when you read.

___ Sample Exercise _____

Mosquitoes love people. Think about that fact the next time you bring your large, heavy hand down on one of their frail little bodies. After you have thought for a moment, go ahead and slap that mosquito. But slap it with respect. According to fossil records, mosquitoes have been around for more than 40 million years. They were here on Earth long before the first people appeared. They were waiting for us. This makes the mosquito a success story.

Around the world, from the tropics to the Arctic, there are more than three thousand kinds of mosquitoes. You are most likely to meet the *Culex*. It is the female *Culex* that seeks your blood. Without blood, her eggs would not develop, and she would die without carrying on her family line. Of course, your hand can bring a very rapid end to her family line.

1. The tone of this selection is
   a. sad and tragic.
   b. proud and boastful.
   c. humorous and factual.
   d. nervous and fearful.

2. The tone of the sentence "Think about that fact the next time you bring your large, heavy hand down on one of their frail little bodies" is
   a. deadly serious.   c. sympathetic.
   b. threatening.   d. sarcastic.

3. The writer's purpose in writing this selection is to
   a. alarm and warn the reader.
   b. entertain and inform the reader.
   c. flatter the reader.
   d. caution the reader.

4. Underline a sentence in which the writer treats mosquitoes as characters with distinct personalities.

Answers and Explanations

1. To complete this sentence, think about your own reactions to the passage. You should see that it is serious in parts but humorous overall.

The best answer is *c*. The tone of the selection is humorous and factual. Each sentence either creates humor or states a fact, so all the sentences support this answer.

The writer creates humor in three ways. First, the writer makes the mosquito seem almost human by giving it the ability to feel and think: "Mosquitoes love people" and "They were waiting for us."

Second, the writer creates humor by stretching the truth, or exaggerating: "Slap it with respect" and "This makes the mosquito a success story."

The writer also creates humor with exaggerated contrast. Whenever one thing is made to seem very different from something else, contrast is used. Contrast can be funny: "Think about that fact the next time you bring your large, heavy hand down on one of their frail little bodies." The great size difference (contrast) between the mosquito and a human hand creates humor.

Two sentences in the first paragraph and most of the sentences in the last paragraph are factual. We learn, for example, that the mosquito has been on Earth for more than 40 million years. We also learn that mosquitoes are found everywhere on Earth and that more than three thousand kinds exist.

Answer *a* is wrong because, although the writer does talk about the death of the mosquito, he or she does not create a sad or tragic tone. The death of insects is not described as a tragic event.

Answer *b* is wrong because the author does not brag or show pride.

Answer *d* is wrong because the writer's attitude is just the opposite of fear. The author has a lighthearted attitude toward the mosquito.

2. Again, use your reaction to help you recognize the tone. Do you take the sentence seriously? Does it seem threatening? Does the writer really seem sympathetic to the mosquito? No. The best answer is *d*. The sentence is sarcastic. It says one thing but means another. The writer is on your side, not the mosquito's.

Answer *a* is incorrect because we can see from the rest of the passage that the writer does not have a serious attitude.

Answer *b* is incorrect because the writer does not emphasize the dangers of mosquitoes.

Answer *c* is incorrect because the writer is not on the side of the mosquito.

3. In completing this sentence, you have to interpret the tone to see what it shows about the author's purpose. Think about the tone. It is mostly humorous. The purpose most likely behind a humorous tone is entertainment. The tone is partly factual. The purpose behind a factual tone is to inform.

The best answer is *b*. The writer's purpose is to entertain and inform the reader. The writer entertains the reader through humor and informs the reader through facts.

Answer *a* is wrong because the writer is not worried about mosquitoes. Thus, he or she is not trying to alarm or warn the reader about anything.

Answer *c* is wrong because the writer does not try to praise or "win over" the reader.

Answer *d* is wrong because the writer does not caution the reader. There are reasons to warn people about mosquitoes, but they are not mentioned.

4. Skim the passage to find sentences in which the mosquito is treated as a character. Look for sentences in which the mosquito is like a person. Two sentences are correct answers.

Mosquitoes love people; *or,* They were waiting for us.

If you had trouble answering these questions, review the sample exercise and questions. If, after that, you still do not understand the answers and the reasons for them, check with your teacher before going on.

PART FOUR

Practice Exercises

- The twenty practice exercises that follow will help you put to use your ability to recognize tone.

- Each exercise is just like the sample exercise you completed in Part Three.

- Read each passage well. Answer carefully and thoughtfully the four questions with it.

- Correct your answers using the Answer Key at the back of the book. Mark your scores on the chart on page 64 before going on to the next exercise.

Practice Exercise *1*

A baby is being born in the Sahara night. We are near a lonely desert well in Niger. The mother has been crying out in pain for hours.

I cannot sleep, and I can see that my friends cannot sleep either. They have their eyes on the black velvet sky. A full moon has just popped above the dark horizon.

Lying near me on the soft sand are my 15-year-old daughter and 13-year-old son. A little farther off our guides are awake. We all can hear the woman cry out. We know that her time to give birth is near, but there are no doctors to help her. She has no husband here to comfort her. We all pray that the mother and child will live.

1. The author establishes a mood of
   a. happiness.
   b. worry.
   c. excitement.
   d. boredom.

2. The writer seems to want to interest
   a. only people who travel a great deal.
   b. nurses who are studying methods of childbirth.
   c. scientists who study human behavior.
   d. anyone interested in human drama.

3. The narrator feels
   a. loving and joyful.
   b. concerned and sad.
   c. eager and energetic.
   d. calm and composed.

4. Underline a sentence that shows that the others in the camp share the narrator's feelings.

Practice Exercise **2**

Newsboys were shouting, "Break with Germany near! Wilson says U-boats must stop attacks!" But the large crowds gathered in Washington, D.C., that day in 1916 did not hear. All eyes were on a block-and-tackle rig on the Munsey Building. It was slowly raising into the air a man in a straitjacket—head down! When he was 100 feet (about 30 meters) above the street, a signal was given. Men pulled out their watches. They looked at the man. Then they looked at their watches. Then they looked at the man, and so on.

After two minutes and thirty seconds, the straitjacket was off. Cheers went up as it fell to the ground.

The man was Harry Houdini. No locks or chains or jails could hold him. Although many people have tried to copy his stunts, Houdini still remains the king of escape.

1. The newsboys were trying to sell papers by creating a mood of
   a. tension.
   b. cheerfulness.
   c. tragedy.
   d. adventure.

2. In the first paragraph the author creates a mood of mounting
   a. relief.
   b. hope.
   c. suspense.
   d. disgust.

3. In this selection the writer uses tone to
   a. create sympathy for performers.
   b. impress the reader with the skill of Houdini.
   c. delight the reader with memories of the past.
   d. show everyone the dangers of foolish action.

4. Underline the sentence that shows the writer's attitude toward Houdini's talent.

Practice Exercise 3

You know what the middle of a summer afternoon in the country can be like. Maybe a rooster crows far off. You hear it, but it seems lost in the stillness. As soon as the sound is gone, you don't believe it ever happened. That was the way it was, day after day, at my aunt's house in the summer. If I walked down the road toward the pike, just to see if anything might be passing, the dust was so thick in the lane I didn't make any more sound than a ghost. If some bird or animal moved back in the brush, it would scare me. This was, of course, when I was little.

I would always come back to the farmhouse in the late afternoon and sit by the window in the parlor and stare at the big oak tree in the front yard. It would be a big event if a leaf fell to the ground.

1. At his or her aunt's house, the writer felt a mood of
   a. noise and confusion.
   b. boredom.
   c. wonder and hope.
   d. caution.

2. The writer mentions a ghost in order to
   a. set a tone of suspense.
   b. add an element of fright.
   c. bring in a note of horror.
   d. deepen a mood of silence.

3. The tone of the final sentence suggests that the writer was
   a. often bored.
   b. a very moody child.
   c. interested in nature.
   d. usually in trouble.

4. Underline a sentence in which exaggeration is used to create tone.

Practice Exercise 4

Possibly someday you will visit England. If you do, you will most certainly go to see the Tower of London. There, among other things, you will see Britain's "royal ravens." These six black birds are a law unto themselves. Their behavior is outrageous. They don't like tourists. They peck putty out of tower window frames. They tear up the grass on the Tower Green. They attack dogs and cats and steal candy from children. They perform whatever other mischief pops into their dark heads.

Anyone else who behaved like that would be kicked out, but not these sassy birds. No one would dream of chasing them away. That's because they are "VIBs" (Very Important Birds). By royal order, the first ravens were brought to the tower in the 1600s. The same royal decree forbids anyone to take their offspring away. They are thought to bring luck to the tower, despite their nastiness.

1. The tone of the selection as a whole is
   a. indignant.
   b. flattering.
   c. tongue-in-cheek.
   d. gloomy.

2. The writer views the ravens with
   a. great admiration.
   b. deep regret.
   c. shocked outrage.
   d. mild disapproval.

3. The writer seems to feel that the ravens
   a. should be evicted from the tower.
   b. are of no interest to anyone anymore.
   c. are an amusing nuisance.
   d. pose a threat to the tourist trade.

4. Underline a sentence in the second paragraph that mocks people who expect special treatment because of their status.

Practice Exercise 5

The Stanley steamer was one of the greatest automobiles
ever made. The demand for the car, however, was never
very great. In fact, few were made. Only 42 of the Series E
model, the last and best, were made during the 1920s. The
main reason for the poor sales record was the high price tag.
The chassis alone cost $6,800, and complete cars sold for
as much as $11,200. But they were worth the high price.
The "motor" was guaranteed for 100,000 miles (160,000
kilometers), and the chassis was guaranteed for three years.
Still, the Stanley was too expensive for most Americans.
The Stanley did not have an attractive design either. It
looked quite boxy and square to most people, while
gasoline-engine cars were sleek and sporty-looking.

1. In this selection, the writer
   a. rages with anger.
   b. uses words of praise.
   c. boasts about personal accomplishments.
   d. shows deep jealousy.

2. In this paragraph, the writer uses tone mostly to
   a. emphasize personal opinions.
   b. exaggerate the real facts.
   c. tell about the opinions of others.
   d. discuss the attitudes of most people.

3. The writer expects the reader to be
   a. amused and intrigued.
   b. confused and annoyed.
   c. concerned and moved.
   d. informed and impressed.

4. Underline two sentences that support the answer to number 1.

___ Practice Exercise **6** ___

At dear old Camp Hi-Wah, we all used a book called *Bird Life for Children*. All the good citizens at Camp Hi-Wah pretended to find the book fascinating. My sister Eileen and I found the book stupid. It was full of horrid pictures in full color of robins and pigeons and redbirds. Under each picture was a dumb paragraph describing how each bird spent its spare time, what it ate, and why children should love it. Eileen and I hated the book. In fact, we hated birds. When we started off on our first bird walk, we had no idea what we were going to suffer that whole awful summer because of our feathered friends. The other campers already knew many birds, but the only bird I knew was the vulture. Cousin Joe took me to a zoo once, and there was a big, fat vulture there. They fed him six rats every day. I kept a sharp eye out for a vulture all summer, but one never turned up at Camp Hi-Wah.

1. The tone of the selection is
    a. serious.
    b. confused.
    c. forceful.
    d. sarcastic.

2. From the narrator's description of Camp Hi-Wah, we can tell that she and her sister found the camp
    a. charming.
    b. frightening.
    c. annoying.
    d. delightful.

3. The tone of the selection indicates that the narrator is
    a. critical but lighthearted.
    b. angry and headstrong.
    c. serious and observant.
    d. anxious and easily upset.

4. Underline a sentence that reveals the narrator's attitude toward the other girls at Camp Hi-Wah.

Practice Exercise 7

As a native North Dakotan, I have learned to live with the cold. When the mercury starts banging away at the bottom of the tube, I tell myself that cold is only a state of mind. It is just the absence of heat. It is a figment of some Florida writer's imagination.

Then I put on two pairs of everything. I cover them all with an Alaskan parka. I light my handwarmers and stay in the house.

I also have some knowledge of snow. More than once I have shoveled six feet of the weather bureau's "partly cloudy" off my driveway.

No, North Dakota winters hold no terror for me. I'll tell you what does. It's being a two-car family with a one-car garage. The fights that develop over whose car is going in the garage at night are something to behold.

1. The sentence "It is a figment of some Florida writer's imagination" is meant to be
   a. factual.   c. scientific.
   b. serious.   d. humorous.

2. The second paragraph shows that the writer
   a. likes to be challenged.
   b. takes the cold seriously.
   c. is depressed during the winter.
   d. is fearful of snowstorms.

3. The sentence ". . . I have shoveled six feet of the weather bureau's 'partly cloudy' . . ." shows that the writer
   a. can be sarcastic.
   b. is lazy.
   c. is restless.
   d. can be dishonest.

4. In one paragraph the writer uses a tone of mock fear mixed with humor. Circle that paragraph.

Practice Exercise 8

Some guys will go to any length to prove a point. For instance, a friend of mine was fishing out of Trophy Lodge on Great Bear Lake in far northern Canada a couple of years ago. He said to me, "We were catching fish on anything we threw out. So I put an empty twelve-tablet aspirin tin on a leader, fixed a hook to it, and threw it out. I caught a ten-pound lake trout." I hate to see a guy with a smirk like that on his face.

I thought his story was too good to be true, so this past summer I visited Great Bear Lake to see if I could perform the same feat. I used the head of a golf club that I had painted, some car keys with spots on them, and a plastic toy soldier. Everything caught fish. My biggest was a fifteen-pound laker. I heard later that a group of local boys caught lakers weighing 41, 45, 49, and 55 pounds the same day on bits of junk!

1. At first, the writer viewed his or her friend's story about fishing on Great Bear Lake with
   a. great joy.   c. praise.
   b. no interest.   d. disbelief.

2. The writer's comment that "everything caught fish" is
   a. a serious statement of fact.
   b. an exaggeration to create humor.
   c. a sarcastic remark.
   d. an emotional outburst.

3. The selection ends on a note of
   a. alarm.
   b. defeat.
   c. sorrow.
   d. astonishment.

4. Underline a sentence that shows that the writer didn't appreciate his or her friend's boastful tone.

Practice Exercise 9

For the thrill of catching really big marlin and swordfish, you have to cross over to Cuba and work the Gulf Stream out of Havana. Cuba is 90 miles (more than 140 kilometers) from Key West, and, in a good year, the fishing begins in mid-April and lasts through September.

However, there is one problem—restrictions limit travel between the United States and Cuba. You can still fish off Key West, though. If you're lucky, you can land prize marlin and swordfish right in the harbor!

During the afternoon and evening, the sweet, sad, fishy smell of the Atlantic trade winds blows over Key West. It cools the air and rustles the leaves of the coconut palms. The mornings are stifling, and you can pan-fry fish in the noonday sun on South Street.

1. In which sentence is tone developed by exaggeration?
  a. To catch really big marlin and swordfish, you have to cross over to Cuba and work the Gulf Stream out of Havana.
  b. Cuba is 90 miles (more than 140 kilometers) from Key West, and, in a good year, the fishing begins in mid-April and lasts through September.
  c. Large marlin and swordfish are caught right in the harbor.
  d. The mornings are stifling, and you can pan-fry fish in the noonday sun on South Street.

2. During the evening, Key West is
  a. breezy and cool.
  b. warm and dry.
  c. still and chilly
  d. hot and humid.

3. The writer discusses fishing off Key West in a tone that shows
  a. excitement.   c. caution.
  b. defeat.   d. disappointment.

4. Underline a sentence that supports the answer to number 3.

Practice Exercise *10*

People sometimes ask me why I did not become president of the United States. They think I would make a good president. I have a ready answer to such a question. I point out that I could not possibly become president. Yes, I do have all the legal qualifications: I was born in the United States, and I am over 35. However, I am an only child. No person who was an only child has ever been elected president. The closest anyone came to it was Franklin D. Roosevelt. He had only a half-brother. So he barely made it.

So if you want to become president, don't be an only child. In fact, it helps to come from a large family. Twenty-five of our presidents came from families of five or more children. Seven came from families of ten or more children, and two came from families of twelve children.

1. The writer's answer to the question about not becoming president is
   a. regretful.
   b. angry.
   c. sorrowful.
   d. surprising.

2. The writer's attitude toward the presidency is shown by the use of
   a. inside information about American politics.
   b. the comments of friends.
   c. trivial facts about past presidents.
   d. gloomy predictions of the future.

3. The overall tone of the selection is
   a. mildly humorous.
   b. overly sentimental.
   c. highly emotional.
   d. bitingly sarcastic.

4. Underline a sentence in which the writer gives humorous advice to the reader.

Practice Exercise *11*

The most important thing to remember when you buy a plant for your house is to be sure that you buy an *indoor* plant.

Buying plants is not the same as buying clothes, food, or cars. Probably the most important factor that makes buying plants more chancy is that they do not have brand names. Say what you will, brand names assure us of good quality.

The only way to make up for the lack of brand names is to buy your plants at a nursery. It is risky to buy them at a dime store, a department store, or a supermarket. Generally speaking, those stores are only jumping on the plant bandwagon and have no real interest in the plants or in you. Buy your plants from someone whose business is selling plants.

1. According to the writer, brand names create a feeling of
   a. curiosity.
   b. trust.
   c. caution.
   d. confusion.

2. The writer feels that the attitude in most department stores is one of
   a. security.
   b. wonder.
   c. helplessness.
   d. carelessness.

3. The writer views the subject of buying houseplants with
   a. caution.
   b. anger.
   c. scientific interest.
   d. childish delight.

4. Underline a sentence that supports the correct answer to number 2.

Practice Exercise *12*

At first glance, Cooperstown, New York, seems almost too good to be true. Main Street is lined with two- and three-story brick buildings. You will find no parking meters. You will not find much traffic either, except in midsummer. There are old country stores, small frame houses, vast lawns, and large elms. Best of all, perhaps, are the museums.

The town was founded by Judge William Cooper, father of one of the first American novelists, James Fenimore Cooper. The writer spent much of his youth in the area. He liked to listen to Indian tales, which he later used in his novels. In fact, many of his novels are set in the Cooperstown area.

Cooperstown may *seem* too good to be true. But it is true, and it is there waiting for the visitor to admire its quaint beauty.

1. The writer feels that a town without parking meters
   a. will go broke.
   b. is a better place for not having them.
   c. will have serious traffic problems.
   d. will be overrun with tourists.

2. The mood of Cooperstown may be described as
   a. confused.
   b. peaceful.
   c. busy.
   d. gloomy.

3. The author of this passage views Cooperstown with an attitude of
   a. anger.
   b. distrust.
   c. sympathy.
   d. admiration.

4. One paragraph presents facts in a direct way, without revealing the attitude of the writer. Circle that paragraph.

Practice Exercise *13*

I go back to Detroit about once a year. It always amazes me to see so many Swiss-cheese hulks running around. It strikes me as ironic that here, in the city that produces all those shiny new cars, people put up with the cost, the danger, and the ugliness of rust buckets for their own cars.

Detroit's clunkers aren't *old* cars by any means. If anything, they're middle-aged. By age five, many cars in Detroit show spots and panels that are rusted through. One carmaker said that in Detroit, where salt is used on streets every winter, a car doesn't last more than four years without rust taking its toll.

Forty years ago, the average lifespan of a car was 13.5 years. Today, the average lifespan is between eight and nine years.

1. The writer discusses the car situation in Detroit with a tone of
   a. surprise.
   b. good cheer.
   c. relief.
   d. excitement.

2. The writer's remark about "Swiss-cheese hulks" is meant to be
   a. boastful and conceited.
   b. lively and informative.
   c. sarcastic and critical.
   d. sincere and factual.

3. The comments in the final sentences are
   a. hopeful and happy.
   b. amusing and imaginative.
   c. flattering but untruthful.
   d. factual and unpleasant.

4. In the first paragraph, underline two descriptive names for cars that show the writer's attitude.

Practice Exercise 14

For years I have puzzled over the difficulty of giving and understanding simple directions, especially when traveling. I ask such seemingly easy questions as "Where do I turn off Route 40 for the bypass around St. Louis?" or "How do I get to the museum?" The person whom I ask either says, "I'm a stranger here myself," or gives me the directions I want. The directions always end with "You can't miss it."

About half the time I *do* miss it, thanks to my helpful guide. I turn down High Street instead of Ohio Street. It was six blocks to the turn, not seven. Many people who give directions apparently can't tell the difference between right and left. Others don't say what they mean. You carefully count the next five stoplights before the turn and find that your guide meant that stop *signs* should be counted as stoplights. It is all very frustrating, and someday I may learn to stay home or buy a very detailed map before I venture far from home.

1. The writer's general attitude is mainly one of
a. amusement.
b. fear.
c. frustration.
d. excitement.

2. The writer's attitude toward the people who give directions is one of
a. respect.
b. annoyance.
c. gratitude.
d. sympathy.

3. Judging from the tone, it seems fair to say that the writer
a. takes traveling very seriously.
b. enjoys the most up-to-date gadgets.
c. has a warm sense of humor.
d. enjoys unexpected adventures when traveling.

4. Underline a sentence in the second paragraph in which the writer uses a disapproving tone.

Practice Exercise 15

Exactly what is happiness? According to one expert, it is "a state of mind in which our thinking is pleasant most of the time."

Happiness is an end result. It may come from as many different things as there are stars in the sky. Different people find happiness in different ways.

"Happiness comes from being needed," says the old person.

"Happiness is being loved," says the young person.

"Happiness is being accepted by others and accepting them," says the teenager.

"Happiness comes from helping others," says the Salvation Army soldier.

Happiness doesn't just happen. It is a habit. As Abraham Lincoln once said, "Most people are about as happy as they make up their minds to be."

1. Tone is developed here through
   a. scientific statements.
   b. several long, wordy paragraphs.
   c. flowery, sentimental language.
   d. violent differences of opinion.

2. The writer establishes a tone of
   a. desperate yearning for happiness.
   b. calm thinking about happiness.
   c. lively joking about happy people.
   d. cruel sarcasm toward happy people.

3. The teenager's definition suggests an attitude of
   a. selflessness.
   b. friendship.
   c. adventure.
   d. disappointment.

4. Underline the quotation that sums up the writer's attitude toward happiness.

— Practice Exercise *16* _____

One day in January 1965, a man named H. D. Settel called me on the phone to report a ghost in his apartment on Riverside Drive, New York. Since I also live on that street, it seemed to me that I had no choice but to take the case.

Mr. Settel knew that something was wrong when his wife began acting odd. She often cried for no reason and said she had the strange feeling of wanting to leave her physical body.

One night about midnight, Mrs. Settel sat up in bed and began talking in a foreign language. Her husband turned the light on, which awakened her. She did not know that she had said anything. Later that night a thunderstorm awakened the couple again. As they tried to get back to sleep, they heard the crying of a baby. It came from the wall nearest their bed.

1. The passage creates a mood of
   a. mounting suspense.
   b. mild humor.
   c. excitement and joy.
   d. angry conflict.

2. Over the course of the passage, the narrator's attitude changes from
   a. guilt to happiness.
   b. annoyance to depression.
   c. reluctance to interest.
   d. excitement to boredom.

3. At the end of the passage, the crying of a baby adds an element of
   a. humor.
   b. terror.
   c. sympathy.
   d. concern.

4. Underline the sentence that shows that the author felt obliged to help the couple.

— Practice Exercise **17** ——————————————

A warm, glowing fire in a fireplace can be a comforting thing. Most people think of wood smoke with fond memories of "the good old days." There is a warmth and quaintness in the aroma of burning wood. Beyond that, though, a fireplace has some practical advantages.

It can be a good way to save energy. In spring and fall, a small fire will take away early morning and evening chills without your having to spend a great deal of money on a large heating system.

A fireplace can be important in emergencies. If a power failure stops the normal heating system, you'll be grateful for your fireplace.

1. In the first paragraph, the writer uses descriptive words to create a mood of
   a. happiness and excitement.
   b. wonder and amazement.
   c. coziness and comfort.
   d. worry and concern.

2. The writer mentions "the good old days" to
   a. suggest a feeling of gloom.
   b. link fireplaces with good memories.
   c. excite a spirit of adventure.
   d. develop tension.

3. The overall purpose of the passage is to
   a. tell the reader how to build a fireplace.
   b. persuade the reader to save energy.
   c. make fireplaces seem appealing.
   d. inform the reader about different kinds of fuel.

4. Circle the paragraph that uses a note of caution to suggest that a fireplace may be a necessity, not a luxury.

Practice Exercise *18*

Major league baseball is one of the most difficult of all games. It may not seem so from the stands, but it does when you get out onto the field and take a close look. For instance, the distance between pitcher and catcher is a matter of twenty paces. This seems awfully short when you put a catcher's mitt on and try to catch a ball from a pitcher who throws with the speed and power of the greats. Some catchers wear a sponge in the mitt when working with fastball pitchers. Even this protection and the bulky mitt itself are not enough to rob the ball of shock and sting. The force of the pitch can make your hand lame unless you know how to "ride with the throw" and kill some of its speed. The pitcher, standing on the mound, seems huge and towering from that short distance. When he ties himself into a coiled spring ready to throw, it takes all your self-control not to break and run for shelter.

1. The writer views baseball players with
   a. annoyance.   c. envy.
   b. sarcasm.   d. respect.

2. The description of the pitcher in the last few sentences is designed to make the reader feel
   a. pride.   c. guilt.
   b. fear.   d. disgust.

3. From the tone of the writing, we can see that, in the opinion of the writer, baseball
   a. players are overpaid.
   b. is a boring game.
   c. is not as easy as it looks.
   d. is an exciting game for children.

4. Underline a sentence in which the writer uses a personal tone to emphasize the pitcher's powerful appearance.

Practice Exercise *19*

There is something to be said for a bad education. By any standards, mine was terrible, and I talked about it for years in public and in private. I talked about it as if it were a kind of Purple Heart that both excused my weaknesses and made my mild successes seem even better.

I am not exaggerating. My education really was bad. As a child, I lived on a ranch in Colorado with the nearest one-room schoolhouse four miles away and the roads blocked in winter. Sometimes there was no teacher for the school. Sometimes my brother and I were the only pupils.

It is true that we were a family that read a lot, but my father's books were about history and law. I eagerly read what I could but found a good deal of it impossible to digest.

However, it was at college that I seriously managed to learn nothing. My alma mater was one of those colleges anyone can attend. I did attend and left four years later, untouched by learning.

1. The sentence "However, it was at college that I seriously managed to learn nothing"
    a. has a sarcastic tone.
    b. is strictly factual.
    c. is meant to win the reader's sympathy.
    d. shows the writer's modesty.

2. The tone of the selection as a whole is
    a. cheerful.
    b. uncaring.
    c. impersonal.
    d. personal.

3. The writer began to read the family books
    a. unwillingly.
    b. eagerly.
    c. sadly.
    d. successfully.

4. Underline a sentence in which the writer accepts some of the blame for getting a bad education.

—— Practice Exercise **20** ——————

On the evening of June 22, 1893, Lady Tryon was entertaining two hundred guests at her home in London. Several of the guests, it was said later, clearly saw the familiar figure of Vice Admiral Sir George Tryon at the party. Chatting with Lady Tryon, they mentioned their surprise and pleasure at seeing Sir George. Lady Tryon told them that they were mistaken. Her husband was still on duty as commander-in-chief of the British fleet in the Mediterranean. Lady Tryon herself had visited him just three weeks before.

At the time of Lady Tryon's party, Sir George was dead. The dreadful news, of course, had not yet reached London and would not arrive until early the next morning. That afternoon his flagship, the *Victoria*, had rammed into a battleship. The *Victoria* had sunk, taking Vice Admiral Tryon, twenty-two officers, and more than three hundred men with her.

1. The mood at Lady Tryon's party was
   a. gloomy.
   b. threatening.
   c. suspenseful.
   d. friendly.

2. Guests spoke to Lady Tryon about her husband in tones of
   a. amazement and delight.
   b. sadness and regret.
   c. concern and sympathy.
   d. excitement and fear.

3. The writer expects the tone of the writing to appeal to
   a. scientists who do not believe in ghosts.
   b. researchers who study human behavior.
   c. children who like sea stories.
   d. people who like suspenseful stories.

4. Underline a sentence that supports the answer to number 2.

PART FIVE

Writing Activities

The writing activities that follow will help you understand tone. The activities will also help you use tone in your own writing.

Complete each activity carefully. Your teacher may ask you to work alone or may prefer to have you work with other students. In many cases, you will be asked to write your answers on separate paper. Your teacher may ask you to write those answers in a notebook or journal. Then all your writing activities will be in the same place.

The activities gradually increase in difficulty. Therefore, you should review each completed activity before you begin a new one. Reread the lessons in Parts One and Two (pages 5–17) if you have any questions about tone.

Writing Activity 1

Read the following passage from a speech by Cochise,
"I am alone."

This for a very long time has been the home of my
people; they came from the darkness, few in numbers and
feeble. The country was held by a much stronger and more
numerous people, and from their stone houses we were
quickly driven. We were a hunting people, living on the
animals that we could kill. We came to these mountains
about us; no one lived here, and so we took them for our
home and country. Here we grew from the first feeble band
to be a great people, and covered the whole country as the
clouds cover the mountains. Many people came to our
country. First the Spanish, with their horses and their iron
shirts, their long knives and guns, great wonders to my
simple people. We fought some, but they never tried to
drive us from our homes in these mountains. After many
years the Spanish soldiers were driven away and the
Mexicans ruled the land. With these little wars came, but we
were now a strong people and we did not fear them. At last
in my youth came the white man, your people. Under the
counsels of my grandfather, who had for a very long time
been the head of the Apaches, they were received with
friendship. Soon their numbers increased and many passed
through my country to the great waters of the setting sun.

A. On a separate piece of paper or in your writing notebook, answer each of the following questions. Your teacher may ask you to discuss your answers with the class.

1. Cochise gave this speech in 1872 to the Americans during the negotiations to move his people to reservations. What message is given in this speech?

2. Imagine that you are hearing this speech. How would Cochise's voice sound? What expression would he have on his face?

B. Choose four words that describe your mood after reading the passage. Write the words on a separate piece of paper or in your writing notebook. Compare your list with a list written by another student. How are the lists similar? How are they different?

Writing Activity 2

Read the following passage from *Daisy Miller: A Study* by Henry James. In the story, Winterbourne has just stopped in the garden of a Swiss hotel.

> It was a beautiful summer morning, and in whatever fashion the young American looked at things, they must have seemed to him charming. He had come from Geneva the day before, by the little steamer, to see his aunt, who was staying at the hotel—Geneva having been for a long time his place of residence. But his aunt had a headache—his aunt had almost always a headache—and now she was shut up in her room, smelling camphor, so that he was at liberty to wander about. He was some seven-and-twenty years of age; when his friends spoke of him, they usually said that he was at Geneva, "studying." When his enemies spoke of him they said—but, after all, he had no enemies; he was an extremely amiable fellow, and universally liked.

A.   On a separate piece of paper or in your writing notebook, answer each of the following questions. Your teacher may ask you to discuss your answers with the class.

1. What words in the passage hint that the garden is a pleasant place?

2. How does Winterbourne feel about his aunt's illness upon his arrival? What kind of person is Winterbourne? How can you tell?

3. What is the mood of the passage? How does it make you feel?

B. Choose a place that you are fond of. The place might be a room in your house, a local park, a public building, or a place you have visited. On a separate piece of paper or in your writing notebook, list three things that you like about the place. Then list three feelings you have about the place.

Use your lists to help you write a short paragraph about the place. Try to use words that describe the place in a way that shows how you feel about it. Your teacher may ask you to share your paragraph with the class.

Writing Activity 3

Read the following passage from a news article in the *Boston Transcript* as recorded in *Up From Slavery* by Booker T. Washington.

The core and kernel of yesterday's great noon meeting in honor of the Brotherhood of Man, in Music Hall, was the superb address of the Negro President of Tuskegee. "Booker T. Washington received his Harvard A.M. last June, the first of his race," said Governor Wolcott, "to receive an honorary degree from the oldest university in the land, and this for the wise leadership of his people." When Mr. Washington rose in the flag-filled, enthusiasm-warmed, patriotic, and glowing atmosphere of Music Hall, people felt keenly that here was the civic justification of the old abolition spirit of Massachusetts; in his person the proof of her ancient and indomitable faith; in his strong thought and rich oratory, the crown and glory of the old war days of suffering and strife. The scene was full of historic beauty and deep significance. "Cold" Boston was alive with the fire that is always hot in her heart for righteousness and truth. Rows and rows of people who are seldom seen at any public function, whole families of those who are certain to be out of town on a holiday, crowded the place to overflowing. The city was at her birthright *fête* in the persons of hundreds of her best citizens, men and women whose names and lives stand for the virtues that make for honorable civic pride.

A. On a separate piece of paper or in your writing notebook, answer each of the following questions. Your teacher may ask you to discuss your answers with the class.

1. What point of view is shown by the tone of the news article?

2. How does the reporter reveal his emotions or attitudes in the article? Find words and/or sentences to support your answers.

3. List three words or phrases that create vivid, or clear, pictures in your mind. Why were those words used? How do they contribute to the mood of the passage?

B. Have you attended an award ceremony or a patriotic event? What event took place? What sounds did you hear? What smells were in the air? On a separate piece of paper or in your writing notebook, make a list of your ideas. Then write a short paragraph about your experience. Ask another student to read your paragraph. Then ask him or her to list three words that describe the paragraph's mood. Do you agree with the student's word choice? Why or why not?

Writing Activity 4

Read the passage from *The Awakening* by Kate Chopin.

Mr. Pontellier, unable to read his newspaper with any degree of comfort, arose with an expression and an exclamation of disgust. He walked down the gallery and across the narrow "bridges" which connected the Lebrun cottages one with the other. He had been seated before the door of the main house. The parrot and the mocking-bird were the property of Madame Lebrun, and they had the right to make all the noise they wished. Mr. Pontellier had the privilege of quitting their society when they ceased to be entertaining.

He stopped before the door of his own cottage, which was the fourth one from the main building and next to the last. Seating himself in a wicker rocker which was there, he once more applied himself to the task of reading the newspaper. The day was Sunday; the paper was a day old. The Sunday papers had not yet reached Grand Isle. He was already acquainted with the market reports, and he glanced restlessly over the editorials and bits of news which he had not had time to read before quitting New Orleans the day before.

Mr. Pontellier wore eye-glasses. He was a man of forty, of medium height and rather slender build; he stooped a little. His hair was brown and straight, parted on one side. His beard was neatly and closely trimmed.

Once in a while he withdrew his glance from the newspaper and looked about him. There was more noise than ever over at the house. The main building was called "the house," to distinguish it from the cottages. The chattering and whistling birds were still at it.

A. On a separate piece of paper or in your writing notebook, answer each of the following questions. Your teacher may ask you to discuss your answers with the class.

1. What was Mr. Pontellier trying to do?

2. What disturbed Mr. Pontellier? What can you tell about his mood?

B. Choose an event from your own experience when you wanted to do something but there were too many distractions. On a separate piece of paper or in your writing notebook, list what you wanted to do and what distractions there were.

Use your lists to help you write a short paragraph about your experience. Compare your experience to Mr. Pontellier's. Try to use words that describe your feelings about the experience.

Writing Activity 5

Read the following poem "The Children's Hour" by Henry
Wadsworth Longfellow.

Between the dark and the daylight,
   When the night is beginning to lower,
Comes a pause in the day's occupations,
   That is known as the Children's Hour.

I hear in the chamber above me
   The patter of little feet,
The sound of a door that is opened
   And voices soft and sweet.

From my study I see in the lamplight,
   Descending the broad hall stair,
Grave Alice, and laughing Allegra,
   And Edith with golden hair.

A whisper, and then a silence:
   Yet I know by their merry eyes
They are plotting and planning together
   To take me by surprise.

A sudden rush from the stairway,
   A sudden raid from the hall!
By three doors left unguarded
   They enter my castle wall.

A.   On a separate piece of paper or in your writing notebook, answer each of the following questions. Use the dictionary to look up any unfamiliar words. Your teacher may ask you to discuss your answers with the class.

1. How does the poet feel about the children in the poem? What words hint at his feelings?

2. According to the poem, when is the "children's hour"? What are the children planning to do?

3. How does the description of the children and their activities add to the mood of the poem?

B.   Choose a person to write about. Decide how you feel about the person. How would you describe the person's looks and actions? What words would you choose to show your feelings about the person? On a separate piece of paper or in your writing notebook, make a list of your ideas. Then use your list to help you write a short poem about the person. Choose words that create pictures, just as Longfellow does in his poem. Your poem does not have to rhyme. Ask another student in the class to read your poem. Then ask the student to describe the tone of the poem. Does the student describe the tone in the same way that you do?

Writing Activity 6

Read the following poem "Solitudes" by Ellen Wheeler
Wilcox.

> Laugh, and the world laughs with you;
>   Weep, and you weep alone,
> For the sad old earth must borrow its mirth,
>   But has trouble enough of its own.
> Sing, and the hills will answer;
>   Sigh, it is lost on the air.
> The echoes bound to a joyful sound,
>   But shrink from voicing care.

On a separate piece of paper or in your writing notebook,
answer each of the following questions. Use the dictionary
to look up any unfamiliar words. Your teacher may ask
you to discuss your answers with the class.

1. What do the words *weep* and *mirth* mean?

2. How does the poet show her feelings, attitudes, and point
   of view in the poem to establish the tone of the poem? Give
   examples.

ANSWER KEY

Practice Exercise 1

1. b   2. d   3. b

4. I cannot sleep, and I can see that my friends cannot sleep either; *or,* We all pray that the mother and child will live.

Practice Exercise 2

1. a   2. c   3. b

4. Although many people have tried to copy his stunts, Houdini still remains the king of escape.

Practice Exercise 3

1. b   2. d   3. a

4. If I walked down the road toward the pike, just to see if anything might be passing, the dust was so thick in the lane I didn't make any more sound than a ghost; *or,* It would be a big event if a leaf fell to the ground.

Practice Exercise 4

1. c   2. d   3. c

4. That's because they are "VIBs" (Very Important Birds).

Practice Exercise 5

1. b   2. a   3. d

4. The Stanley steamer was one of the greatest automobiles ever made; *or,* But they were worth the high price.

Practice Exercise 6

1. d   2. c   3. a

4. All the good citizens at Camp Hi-Wah pretended to find the book fascinating.

Practice Exercise 7

1. d   2. b   3. a

4. The last paragraph should be circled.

Practice Exercise 8

1. d   2. a   3. d
4. I hate to see a guy with a smirk like that on his face.

Practice Exercise 9

1. d   2. a   3. a
4. If you're lucky, you can land prize marlin and swordfish right in the harbor!

Practice Exercise 10

1. d   2. c   3. a
4. So if you want to become president, don't be an only child.

Practice Exercise 11

1. b   2. d   3. a
4. Generally speaking, those stores are only jumping on the plant bandwagon and have no real interest in the plants or in you.

Practice Exercise 12

1. b   2. b   3. d
4. The second paragraph should be circled.

Practice Exercise 13

1. a   2. c   3. d
4. Swiss-cheese hulks; rust buckets

Practice Exercise 14

1. c   2. b   3. a
4. About half the time I do miss it, thanks to my helpful guide; *or,* Many people who give directions apparently can't tell the difference between right and left; *or,* Others don't say what they mean.

Practice Exercise 15

1. c   2. b   3. b

4. "Most people are about as happy as they make up their minds to be."

Practice Exercise 16

1. a   2. c   3. b

4. Since I also live on that street, it seemed to me that I had no choice but to take the case.

Practice Exercise 17

1. c   2. b   3. c

4. The last paragraph should be circled.

Practice Exercise 18

1. d   2. b   3. c

4. When he ties himself into a coiled spring ready to throw, it takes all your self-control not to break and run for shelter.

Practice Exercise 19

1. a   2. a   3. b

4. I talked about it as if it were a kind of Purple Heart that both excused my weaknesses and made my mild successes seem even better.

Practice Exercise 20

1. d   2. a   3. d

4. Chatting with Lady Tryon, they mentioned their surprise and pleasure at seeing Sir George.

PROGRESS CHART

Practice Exercise Number	Put an X through the number of each question answered correctly.				Total Number Correct
	Question	Question	Question	Question	
1	1	2	3	4	
2	1	2	3	4	
3	1	2	3	4	
4	1	2	3	4	
5	1	2	3	4	
6	1	2	3	4	
7	1	2	3	4	
8	1	2	3	4	
9	1	2	3	4	
10	1	2	3	4	
11	1	2	3	4	
12	1	2	3	4	
13	1	2	3	4	
14	1	2	3	4	
15	1	2	3	4	
16	1	2	3	4	
17	1	2	3	4	
18	1	2	3	4	
19	1	2	3	4	
20	1	2	3	4	

Total of correct answers for all 20 exercises:

Rating: 70–80 Excellent
55–69 Good
40–54 Fair